SPOTLIGHT ON THE CIVIL RIGHTS MOVEMENT™

THE MURDER OF EMMETT TILL

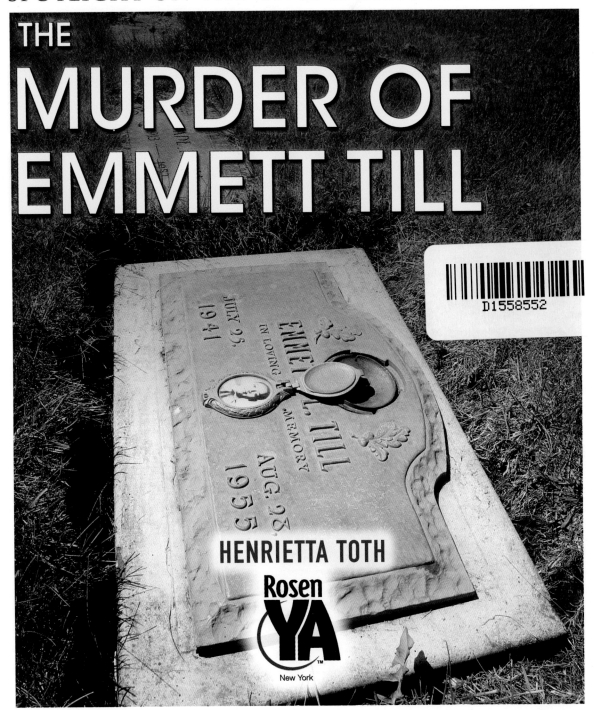

HENRIETTA TOTH

Rosen
YA™
New York

Published in 2018 by The Rosen Publishing Group, Inc.
29 East 21st Street, New York, NY 10010

First Edition

Library of Congress Cataloging-in-Publication Data

Names: Toth, Henrietta, author.
Title: The murder of Emmett Till / Henrietta Toth.
Description: New York : Rosen Publishing, 2018. | Series: Spotlight on the civil rights movement | Includes bibliographical references and index. | Audience: Grades 5–10.
Identifiers: LCCN 2017020367| ISBN 9781538380574 (library bound) | ISBN 9781538380543 (pbk.) | ISBN 9781538380550 (6 pack)
Subjects: LCSH: Till, Emmett, 1941–1955—Juvenile literature. | Mississippi—Race relations—Juvenile literature. | Lynching—Mississippi—History—20th century—Juvenile literature. | African Americans—Crimes against—Mississippi—History—20th century—Juvenile literature. | African American teenage boys—Mississippi—Biography—Juvenile literature. | Racism—Mississippi—History—20th century—Juvenile literature. | Trials (Murder)—Mississippi—Juvenile literature. | Civil rights movements—Southern States—History—20th century—Juvenile literature. | African Americans—Civil rights—Southern States—History—20th century—Juvenile literature.
Classification: LCC E185.93.M6 T68 2018 | DDC 364.1/34—dc23
LC record available at https://lccn.loc.gov/2017020367

Manufactured in the United States of America

On the cover: The circumstances of Emmett Till's murder brought to light for many Americans the persistent danger, oppression, and fear that African Americans in the South lived with on a daily basis—and inspired a widespread movement to end discrimination.

CONTENTS

A BOY FROM CHICAGO

Emmett Louis Till was born in Chicago, Illinois, on July 25, 1941. He was called Bobo, or Bo. When Emmett was six years old, he contracted polio. He survived the disease, but it left him with a stutter. Emmett lived with his mother, Mamie Till-Mobley. He never knew his father, Louis Till, who was executed for misconduct while serving in the US Army.

In 1955, Emmett Till was a fourteen-year-old African American boy growing up on the South Side of Chicago. Like any child, he was looking forward to summer vacation. In August, he went to visit relatives in Mississippi, where he became the victim of a brutal hate crime. Emmett was kidnapped and

Emmett Till is photographed relaxing on his bed. In the summer of 1955, Emmett was looking forward to visiting relatives in Mississippi.

killed by two white men who believed that he had flirted with one of their wives. His murder helped ignite the growing civil rights movement.

A FUN-LOVING TEENAGER

Emmett Till was a happy teenager with a sense of adventure. His cousin Wheeler Parker Jr. remembered that Emmett was outgoing and liked to play pranks. Another cousin, Simeon Wright, said it was hard to tell when Emmett was serious because he liked to joke and make people laugh.

Emmett lived in a middle-class African American neighborhood where he enjoyed playing stickball in the streets. He attended an all-African-American grammar school. Because Emmett was a large boy and strong, some people thought he was older than fourteen. Other people described Emmett as chubby.

Mamie Till-Mobley, Emmett's mother, recalled that her son was loving and clever. He helped with chores at home while she worked long hours to support them. Emmett liked to cook, especially pork chops. She was proud of the young man that Emmett was becoming.

This portrait of Emmett Till shows a happy teenager. Emmett's friends and family recall that he had a lively personality.

VACATION IN MISSISSIPPI

n the summer of 1955, Emmett talked his mother into letting him visit relatives in the Mississippi Delta. She had wanted Emmett to go with her on a road trip west. Reluctantly, she put Emmett aboard a train heading south on August 20. Before Emmett left, his mother gave him his father's signet ring.

Emmett arrived in Money, Mississippi, and stayed at the home of his great-uncle Mose Wright and his cousin Simeon Wright. Uncle Mose was a cotton sharecropper. Emmett and his cousins picked cotton under the summer sun, where hot breezes carried the sweet aroma of honeysuckle flowers.

Emmett had visited his Mississippi relatives before, when he was a small child. Now as a teenager, he had to be aware of race relations in the South. His mother had warned him that life for African Americans in the South was not the same as in the North.

Mose Wright, Emmett Till's great-uncle, is shown whittling some wood outside the courthouse where Emmett's abductors stood trial. Emmett stayed at his uncle's house while visiting Mississippi.

THE SOUTH IN THE 1950s

I n the 1950s, life in the South was different from life in the North. The North was more urban and industrialized, while the South carried on a farm-based existence steeped in old traditions that went back to the Civil War era or before. Many African Americans were sharecroppers on cotton fields owned by whites. Southern society was racially segregated with Jim Crow laws. Public areas, such as diners and theaters, had separate sections for use by whites and blacks. Schools also were segregated, and African Americans regularly experienced abuse, oppression, and racism.

A burning cross was a symbol of intimidation used by the Ku Klux Klan. They would set fire to a cross near the homes or businesses of those they wished to threaten.

The Mississippi Delta that Emmett Till visited is in the north-west part of the state. The Ku Klux Klan was active in the area and terrorized African American residents. In separate instances, two African American men were shot and killed after trying to vote in the spring of 1955. No arrests were made in either crime.

TRIP TO BRYANT'S GROCERY

On August 24, 1955, Emmett Till, his cousins Wheeler Park Jr. and Simeon Wright, and other cousins and friends picked cotton all day in the hot sun. Then the group of eight drove into Money, Mississippi, to buy refreshments. They went to Bryant's Grocery and Meat Market, which catered to African American sharecroppers and their families. Roy and Carolyn Bryant, a young, poor, white couple, owned the store.

Emmett bought two cents worth of bubble gum. Some of the children said they heard Emmett whistle at Carolyn Bryant on his way out of the store. Simeon Wright thought that Emmett

Local residents boycotted Bryant's Grocery after the trial ended in acquittal. Under new ownership, the store functioned as a grocery into the 1980s and then fell into disrepair.

whistled to make the other boys laugh. The boys felt afraid and ran to their car. Carolyn Bryant went to her car to retrieve a pistol. Emmett and his cousins decided not to tell Uncle Mose about what happened, and they soon forgot about it.

ABDUCTED AT NIGHT

F our days later, a humid night turned terrifying at Mose
Wright's house. At about 2:30 a.m., a car with its headlights
off coasted down the driveway. Carolyn Bryant's husband,
Roy, and his half-brother, J. W. Milam, stepped out of the car.
Milam carried a flashlight and a pistol, and they banged on the
door to be let in. They pulled Emmett out of bed, ordering him to
put on his clothes. Emmett dressed without a word, asking only
to put on his socks because he never wore shoes without socks.

Mose Wright begged the men not to take Emmett away.
His wife, Elizabeth, offered Bryant and Milam money to leave

Emmett Till was kidnapped from his uncle Mose's house on August 25, 1955. The sharecropper's shack was located on the edge of cotton fields.

Emmett alone. They said that Emmett was not used to southern ways. The men threatened Uncle Mose's life and left with Emmett.

Mose Wright and others drove all around looking for Emmett. He was missing for three days.

THE MURDER

Emmett Till was killed one week after arriving in Mississippi on vacation.

Roy Bryant and J. W. Milam drove Emmett around for a few hours in the back of a truck. Then they took Emmett to a barn, where they beat and tortured him for supposedly flirting with Carolyn Bryant. Next, they drove Emmett to the Tallahatchie River and ordered him to undress. They shot Emmett through the temple and pushed his body into the water. They tied a seventy-pound (thirty-two kilogram) cotton gin fan to Emmett's neck to weigh down his body in the river.

Emmett Till was wearing this ring when his body was found in the Tallahatchie River. The initials L. T. are those of his father.

Three days later, some boys fishing on the riverbank found Emmett's naked and mutilated body. After being tortured and submerged in water, Emmett's face was unrecognizable. Mose Wright identified Emmett's body from his father's ring.

THE FUNERAL

The local sheriff wanted Emmett Till's body to be quickly buried in Mississippi. Mamie Till-Mobley demanded that her only son be shipped home to Chicago for burial. His body was packed in lime in a pine coffin and placed in a crate that was nailed shut. After Emmett's mother saw his body, she insisted on an open-casket wake. Mamie Till-Mobley wanted the world to see the vicious hate crime that was done to her son. She said, "Let the people see what I've seen, because there's no way I could tell this story and give them the visual picture of what my son looked like."

For three days, more than fifty thousand mourners gathered for the wake of Emmett Till. The crowd waited outside in long lines fanning themselves in the summer heat.

Once inside, most mourners were overcome with emotion.

Mourners at Emmett Till's funeral spill into the street around the church. Thousands of mournful and shocked people filed past the open casket.

A flat plaque with a photo marks the grave of Emmett Till in Burr Oak Cemetery in Alsip, Illinois.

Glass covered Emmett's coffin to try to seal in the odor of his decomposing body. Some people felt sick from the smell and the sight of the grotesque corpse and some even fainted. The funeral was held at the Roberts Temple Church of God in Christ.

The wake and funeral became the largest civil rights gathering at the time. African Americans and whites in the North were shocked and angered by the savage tragedy. On September 6, 1955, Emmett Till was buried in Burr Oak Cemetery.

Emmett's funeral put a spotlight on the treatment of African Americans, particularly in the South. Leaders of the National Association for the Advancement of Colored People (NAACP) denounced the murder and called it a lynching. National and international media covered the story. Dutch, French, and German newspapers wrote about the case. Photos of Emmett in the open casket were published in *Jet*, an African American magazine.

THE TRIAL

Roy Bryant and J. W. Milam were arrested on August 29, 1955, for kidnapping Emmett Till. On September 6, both men were indicted by a grand jury for Emmett's kidnapping and murder. They were held without bond and both pleaded innocent. Mississippi governor Hugh White ordered that Bryant and Milam be fully prosecuted for the crime. From outside of Mississippi came widespread appeals for justice.

The trial began on September 19. Carolyn Bryant made the claim that Emmett had flirted with her. Mose Wright, Emmett's great-uncle, identified Bryant and Milam in court as the men who abducted Emmett. Wright gave dramatic testimony of the night Emmett was kidnapped. It was a brave thing for an African American to do in the Mississippi Delta because blacks did not openly accuse whites, especially in a segregated court. Emmett's mother, Mamie Till-Mobley, also confronted her son's accused murderers.

Mamie Till-Mobley, Emmett Till's mother, cries as she recalls the brutal torture and murder of her teenage son.

Accused murderer Roy Bryant sits with his wife, Carolyn, and his two young sons in the courtroom during the trial in Sumner, Mississippi.

Despite convincing evidence, an all-white, all-male jury acquitted Bryant and Milam on September 23. African Americans and women could not serve on juries at that time. Before reaching their verdict, the jurors were warned by the court to think about what the country's Founding Fathers would think if they found Bryant and Milam guilty of murder. The jury decided their verdict in just over an hour, which included a soda break.

African Americans and sympathetic white northerners were outraged at the verdict and called the trial a sham. It drew attention to the difference between southern and northern legal systems, especially the unjust happenings in the South. Newspapers worldwide covered the trial. The German newspaper *Freies Volk* published the story, "The Life of a Negro Isn't Worth a Whistle."

AFTERMATH OF THE MURDER AND TRIAL

Emmett Till's murder and the verdict at the trial had a profound effect on Mose Wright and his family. After the trial ended, the Wright family fled Mississippi for the suburbs of Chicago. The trial ended on Friday, they packed over the weekend, and were gone by Monday.

Four months after the trial ended, Roy Bryant and J. W. Milam gave an interview to *Look* magazine. They were paid $4,000 for the article in which they admitted that they were responsible for Emmett's death. Although they had now confessed to the murder, they could not be brought to trial again because of a

Murder defendants J. W. Milam and Roy Bryant celebrate their acquittal with their wives. A few months later, they admitted their guilt in an article in *Look* magazine.

legal defense called double jeopardy. Double jeopardy prevents a person from being tried for the same crime after a verdict has been issued.

The acquittal of Bryant and Milam moved African Americans to seek changes in the justice system and in civil rights. Many northern whites supported their efforts.

INFLUENCE ON THE CIVIL RIGHTS MOVEMENT

The murder of Emmett Till exposed America's racism, social injustice, inequality, and white supremacy. It had a strong impact on the civil rights movement. African Americans were inspired to take a stand and protest against discrimination and oppression. They sought equal justice and equal rights, especially for African Americans in the South.

Four months after Emmett's murder, Rosa Parks was riding a bus in Montgomery, Alabama. She was supposed to give up her seat to a white man and sit farther back in the black section. Rosa Parks said, "I thought of Emmett Till, and I couldn't go back."

The African American community gathers in protest of the murder of Emmett Till at Sharp Street Methodist Church in Baltimore, Maryland, on September 28, 1955.

Her action spurred the Montgomery bus boycott and the Supreme Court verdict that ended segregation. Protests in support of civil rights erupted in many places. Martin Luther King Jr. emerged as an icon of the civil rights movement. He called Emmett's murder "one of the most brutal and inhuman crimes of the twentieth century."

Nine African American students are escorted by the military from Central High School in Little Rock, Arkansas. It was their second full day of classes at the newly desegregated school.

As the civil rights movement grew, there were more protests, marches, sit-ins, and riots. In 1954, the Supreme Court ruling on *Brown v. Board of Education* was met with protests. The court ruled in favor of racial integration within schools. It was a victory against segregation, but the law was difficult to enforce. In 1957, in Little Rock, Arkansas, a group of African American students called the Little Rock Nine were prevented from entering the newly racially integrated Central High School.

The 1963 March on Washington brought together more than two hundred thousand Americans to protest continuing civil rights challenges. Following the march, Martin Luther King Jr. gave his famous "I Have a Dream" speech.

There were also more victims of civil rights abuse. In 1964, the Freedom Summer murders shocked the nation. Three activists for African American voting rights were killed in Mississippi.

A MOTHER'S MISSION

E mmett Till's murder irrevocably changed his mother's life. Mamie Till-Mobley saw the historic significance in what had happened to her son. She bravely drew attention to Emmett's murder in a time of segregation. She felt she had a responsibility to expose the racial hatred and injustice afflicting Mississippi and the Deep South. Mamie Till-Mobley wanted to show people the horrible things that happened because of racial hatred. She said, "the fact that it happened to a child, that made all the difference in the world."

Mamie Till-Mobley made it her mission that Emmett would not be forgotten. She remained devoted to honoring her son's legacy until she died in 2003. She worked for civil

Mamie Till-Mobley speaks to the crowd at an antilynching rally in Harlem in New York City. The rally took place soon after her son's murderers were acquitted.

rights, speaking at rallies about her son. She spoke of Emmett's difficult birth and his difficult death. She also became a teacher, who influenced hundreds of children.

REOPENING THE CASE

The murder of Emmett Till was not fully investigated in 1955. There was no autopsy, and Emmett's body was identified by the signet ring he wore. Mamie Till-Mobley's request to President Eisenhower for help went unanswered.

In 2004, the case of Emmett's murder was reopened because questions remained. Were more people involved in the murder? Maybe even African Americans? On June 1, 2005, Emmett's body was exhumed to do an autopsy. On June 4, 2005, his body was reburied in a new casket in the same grave at Burr Oak Cemetery in suburban Chicago. The old casket was put on display at the National Museum of African American History and Culture in Washington, DC.

Friends and family leave a prayer service prior to the exhumation of Emmett Till's body from Burr Oak Cemetery in Alsip, Illinois. The FBI reopened the murder case in 2004.

Following an investigation, in 2007 a grand jury decided not to indict Carolyn Bryant or any other accomplices in Emmett Till's murder. Many people reacted strongly to this decision. They felt that not enough had changed since 1955.

TRUTH, LIES, AND CONFESSIONS

Truth, lies, and confessions played a role in the case of the murder of Emmett Till. Simeon Wright, Emmett's cousin, said his father would have sneaked Emmett out of Mississippi if they had told him about the incident at Bryant's Grocery. Emmett's cousins also said that "no one had dared Emmett to flirt with Carolyn Bryant and he never spoke out of turn to her." If Emmett did whistle, it might have been to alleviate his stutter or he might have whistled at the chess game being played outside the store.

Emmet Till's great-uncle Mose Wright, his mother, Mamie Till-Mobley, and his cousin Simeon Wright attend the murder trial in Sumner, Mississippi.

At the murder trial, Carolyn Bryant claimed that Emmett Till had flirted with her and touched her hand. After the case was reopened, she confessed in 2007 that she lied about Emmett flirting with her and that Emmett did nothing to justify what was done to him.

EMMETT TILL'S LEGACY

Emmett Till left a legacy of pain and suffering as the victim of a racist crime. The brutality of his murder did not let people forget the crime. The lynching of a fourteen-year-old boy awakened northerners to the racism that prevailed in the southern half of the country. Emmett's legacy helped spark the civil rights movement and inspired people to stand up to racism and discrimination.

Emmett's legacy encouraged more civil rights protests and marches. The Greensboro Four were black college students who staged a sit-in at a white lunch counter in Greensboro, North Carolina, to protest segregation. In 1965, Martin Luther King Jr.

In March 1965, demonstrators carried American flags in a civil rights march from Selma to Montgomery in Alabama. The march was in support of African American voting rights.

led a march from Selma to Montgomery, Alabama, that led to the passage of the Voting Rights Act.

A troubling legacy of Emmett's murder was also that it incited more hate crimes with more victims. In Birmingham, Alabama, four girls were killed in the bombing of the 16th Street Baptist Church.

REMEMBERING EMMETT TILL

Emmett Till is remembered in many ways beyond the historical fact of his murder. In Chicago, his name is used for a school, the Emmett Louis Till Math and Science Academy, and a street. In 1991, 71st Street was renamed Emmett Till Road. In popular culture, Emmett Till appears in plays, poems, songs, and fiction. Singer and songwriter Bob Dylan wrote the song "The Death of Emmett Till." *A Wreath for Emmett Till* is a book of poetry by Marilyn Nelsen.

A statute to Emmett Till was erected in Denver, Colorado. It is now located in Pueblo, Colorado, and has been defaced several times. In Mississippi, a historical marker identifies the site where Emmett's body was found in the Tallahatchie River. It has been riddled with bullet holes. Another historical sign that tells Emmett's story stands outside Bryant's Grocery. Its panels have been peeled off. The vandalism of Emmett's statue and the historical markers have been investigated as hate crimes. These acts, as well as Emmett's tragic murder, serve to spur on the fight for racial justice today.

A bronze statue of civil rights icons Martin Luther King Jr. and Emmett Till is readied for its dedication ceremony in City Park in Denver, Colorado, in September 1976.

abduct To kidnap or to illegally take away someone.

aftermath The result of an event or series of events.

bond Money paid to release a person from legal custody.

cotton gin A machine that separates the fibers of the cotton plant.

double jeopardy A legal rule that prevents a person from being tried twice for the same crime.

icon A person or thing that is highly respected.

Jim Crow Laws that enforced racial segregation, especially in southern states.

legacy Something important that is handed down from the past.

lynching Death carried out by a mob of people without legal cause.

polio A viral disease that can result in paralysis.

racism Intolerance of another group of people based on race.

segregated Separated based on race or ethnicity.

sham Something that is not as it seems.

sharecropper A tenant farmer who pays a share of his crops as rent.

signet A small seal or mark, as on a ring.

Canadian Museum for Human Rights
85 Israel Asper Way
Winnipeg, MB R3C 0L5
Canada
(204) 289-2000
Website: https://www.humanrights.ca
Facebook: @canadianmuseumforhumanrights
Twitter: @CMHR_News
Instagram: @cmhr_mcdp
This museum explores the topic of human rights through galleries and
    events, especially as it relates to Canadians.

Emmett Till Historic Intrepid Center
33 Thomas Street
Glendora, MS 38928
(662) 375-9304
Website: http://www.glendorams.com
Facebook: @ETHICMuseum
Parts of the Emmett Till story are recreated at this regional museum,
    including the storefront of Bryant's Grocery and the pickup truck used
    to abduct Emmett.

Emmett Till Interpretive Center
120 North Court Street
Sumner, MS 38957
(662) 483-0048
Website: http://www.emmett-till.org
Facebook: @TillCenter
The courthouse where Emmett Till's murderers were tried has been
    restored to its 1955 appearance and helps to tell this tragic story.

National Civil Rights Museum
450 Mulberry Street
Memphis, TN 38103
(901) 521-9699
Website: https://www.civilrightsmuseum.org
Facebook: @NCRMuseum
Twitter: @NCRMuseum
Instagram: @ncrmuseum
Through artifacts, documents, and photographs, this museum covers
    the African American experience from slavery through the civil
    rights movement and beyond.

National Museum of African American History and Culture
14th Street and Constitution Avenue NW
Washington, DC 20001
(202) 633-1000
Website: https://nmaahc.si.edu
Facebook: @NMAAHC
Twitter: @nmaahc.si.edu
Instagram: @nmaahc
The African American journey in American history is the focus at this
    Smithsonian Institution museum.

WEBSITES

Because of the changing nature of internet links, Rosen Publishing has
developed an online list of websites related to the subject of this book.
This site is updated regularly. Please use this link to access this list:

http://www.rosenlinks.com/SCRM/Till

Crowe, Chris. *Getting Away with Murder: The True Story of the Emmett Till Case*. New York, NY: Dial Books for Young Readers, 2003.

Crowe, Chris. *Mississippi Trial, 1955*. New York, NY: Speak–Penguin Random House, 2003.

Hooks, Gwendolyn. *If You Were a Kid During the Civil Rights Movement*. New York, NY: C. Press/F. Watt Trade, 2017.

Hoose, Philip. *Claudette Colvin: Twice Toward Justice*. New York, NY: Square Fish, 2010.

Levine, Ellen S. *Freedom's Children: Young Civil Rights Activists Tell Their Own Stories*. New York, NY: Puffin Books, 2000.

Nelson, Kadir. *Heart and Soul: The Story of America and African Americans*. New York, NY: Balzer + Bray, 2013.

Nelson, Marilyn. *A Wreath for Emmett Till*. New York, NY: HMH Books for Young Readers, 2009.

Pinkney, Andrea Davis. *Sit-In: How Four Friends Stood Up by Sitting Down*. New York, NY: Little, Brown Books for Young Readers, 2010.

Turk, Mary C. *The Civil Rights Movement for Kids: A History with 21 Activities*. Chicago, IL: Chicago Review Press, 2000.

Wright, Simeon, with Herb Boyd. *Simeon's Story: An Eyewitness Account of the Kidnapping of Emmett Till*. Chicago, IL: Chicago Review Press, 2011.

American Experience. "The Murder of Emmett Till," PBS, January 20, 2003. http://www.pbs.org/wgbh/americanexperience/films/till.

Blakemore, Erin. "What the Director of the African American History Museum Says About the New Emmett Till Revelations." Smithsonian .com, February 3, 2017. http://www.smithsonianmag.com /smithsonian-institution/what-director-african-american-history -museum-says-about-new-emmett-till-revvelations-180962025.

Cuba, Darold. "Emmett Till, Whose Martyrdom Launched the Civil Rights Movement." *New York Times*, August 28, 2016. https://www .nytimes.com/interactive/projects/cp/obituaries/archives/emmett-till.

History.com. "Emmett Till." A&E Television Network. Retrieved February 1, 2017. http://www.history.com/topics/black-history/emmett-till.

Latson, Jennifer. "How Emmett Till's Murder Changed the World." *Time*, August 28, 2015. http://time.com/4008545/emmett-till-history.

Parker, Laura. "Civil Rights Museum in Mississippi Arouses Hope—and Distrust." *National Geographic*, June 24, 2014. http://news .nationalgeographic.com/news/2014/06/140623-mississippi -civil-rights-museum-history-freedom-summer.

60 Minutes. "The Murder of Emmett Till." CBS, October 24, 2005. http://www.downvids.net/cbs-60-minutes-emmett-till-part-1 -794699.html.

Till-Mobley, Mamie, and Christopher Benson. *Death of Innocence: The Story of the Hate Crime That Changed America*. New York, NY: Random House, 2011.

Time. "The Law: Trial by Jury." October 3, 1955. http://content.time.com /time/subscriber/article/0,33009,807680,00.html.

Tyson, Timothy B. *The Blood of Emmett Till*. New York, NY: Simon & Schuster, 2017.

About the Author

Henrietta Toth is a writer and editor who has worked on books covering such topics as civil rights, racism, slavery, and social justice. Her research for this volume included recently published material that shed new light on what really happened to Emmett Till.

Photo Credits